Doodle Design & Draw

DREAM ROOMS

Ellen Christiansen Kraft

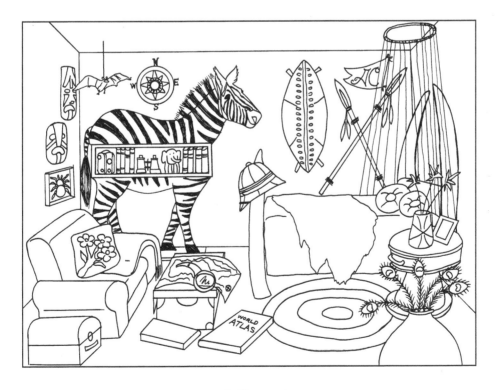

Dover Publications, Inc.
Mineola, New York

Note

Over sixty contemporary designs need some finishing touches before they're ready to be presented to the trendiest contractors and department stores. Just grab a pencil and begin adding color, fabric patterns, accessories, and more to the incomplete furniture and floor plans. Whether you want to design a beautiful bedspread, add detail to the woodwork on a desk, or design an entire room from the ground up, it's all right here in this unique book. Featuring a series of illustrations right out of a modern design magazine, aspiring decorators will love testing their skills with *Doodle, Design & Draw—DREAM ROOMS*.

Pages 1–10 feature a series of nearly complete dream rooms for you to use to experiment with different color combinations, and to provide you with inspiration for your own designs. Pages 11–20 host a catalog of dream room accessories—from dressers and desks, to beds, mirrors, lamps and other flare—useful for experimenting with small detail. Pages 21–51 contain incomplete rooms for you turn into dream rooms. Use your creative imagination to add bedspreads, furniture, and accessories, and give each room a distinct look and style. Finally, on pages 52–69 you will find empty floor plans that will help you design your dream rooms from the ground up! It's up to you to decide where each piece of furniture will sit, what colors you will use, and what kinds of accessories will make the room unique.

The inside covers include sample fabric patterns for extra inspiration.

Copyright

Copyright © 2012 by Dover Publications, Inc.
All rights reserved.

Bibliographical Note

Doodle, Design & Draw—DREAM ROOMS is a new work, first published by Dover Publications, Inc., in 2012.

International Standard Book Number
ISBN-13: 978-0-486-48439-6
ISBN-10: 0-486-48439-4

Manufactured in the United States by Courier Corporation
48439401
www.doverpublications.com

Dream Rooms 1

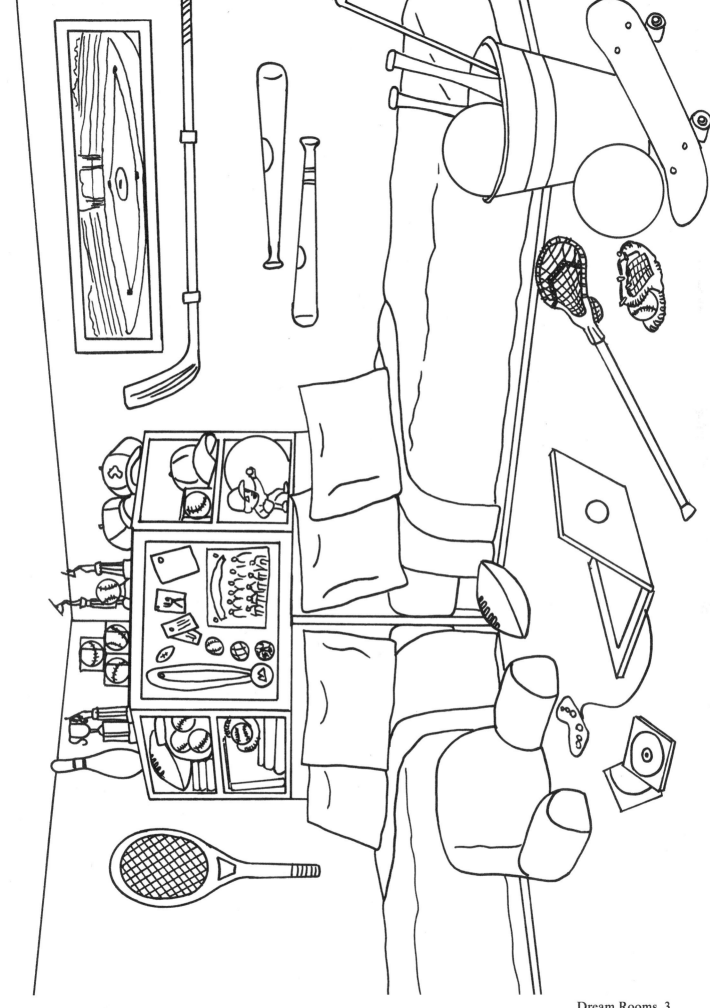

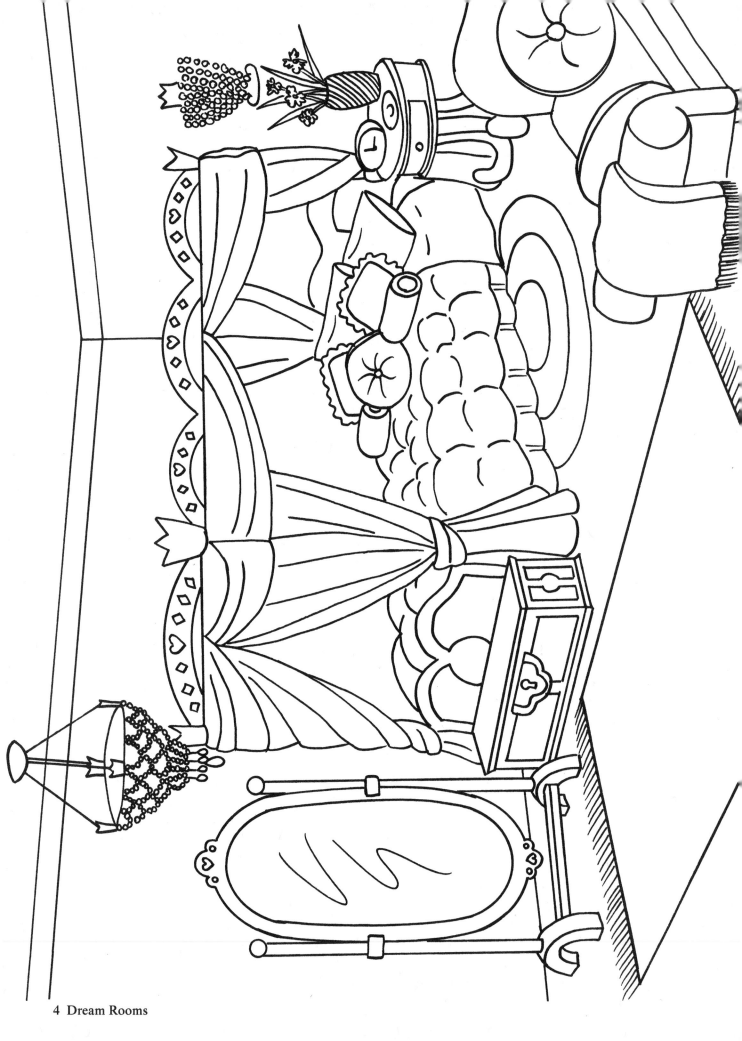

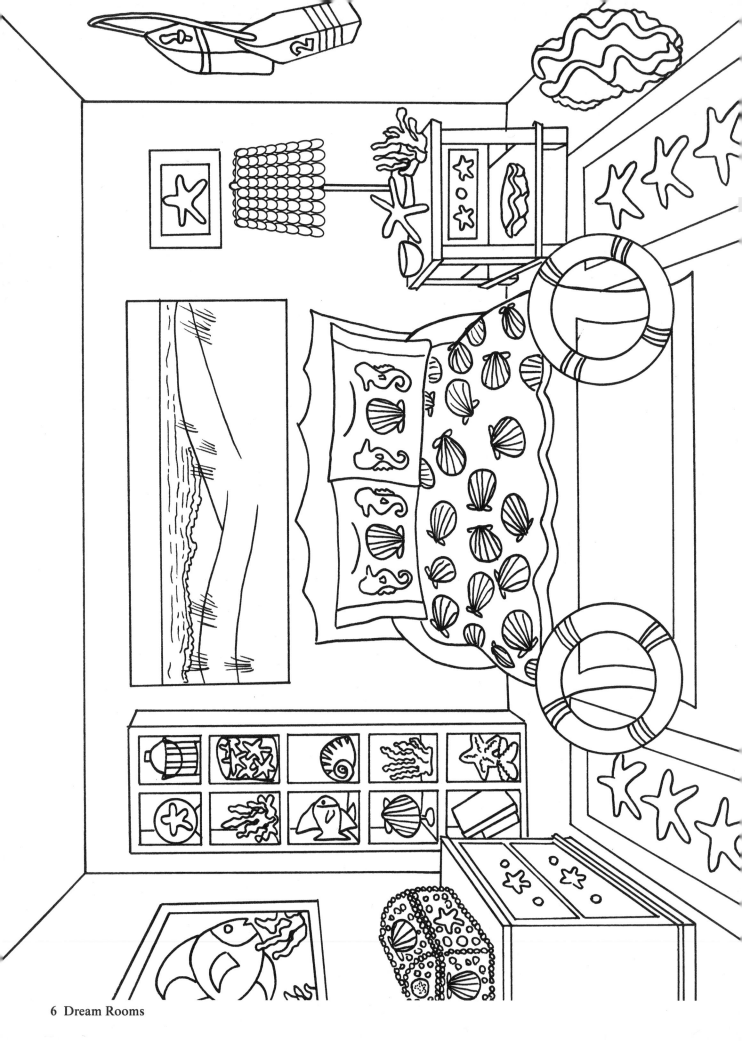

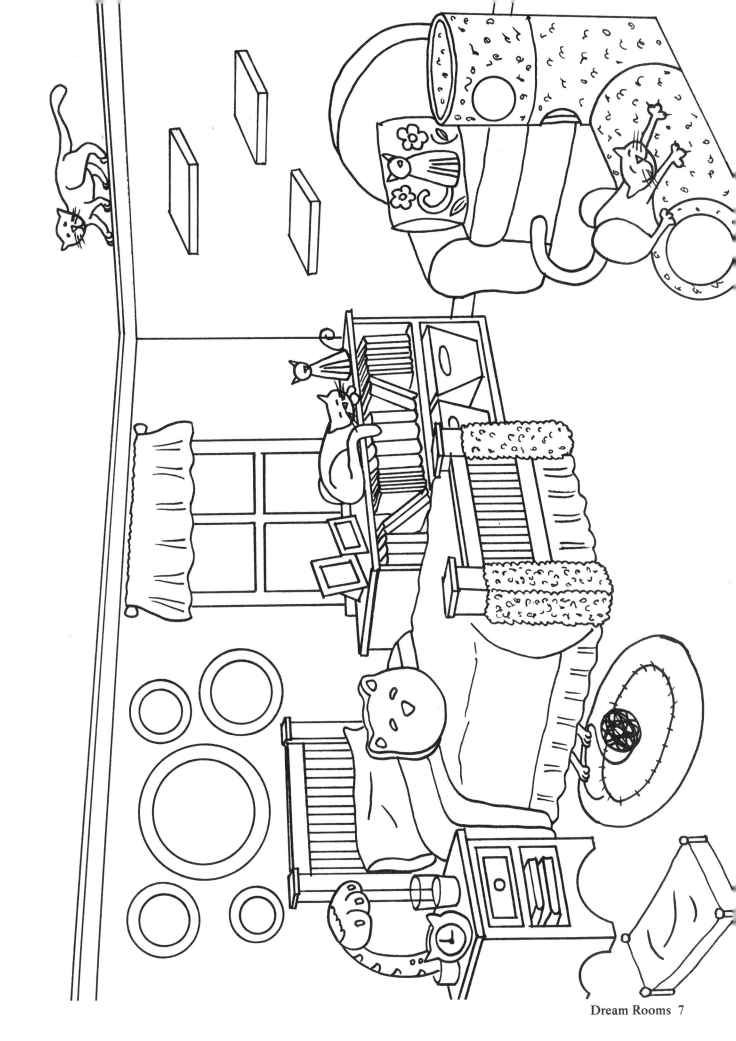

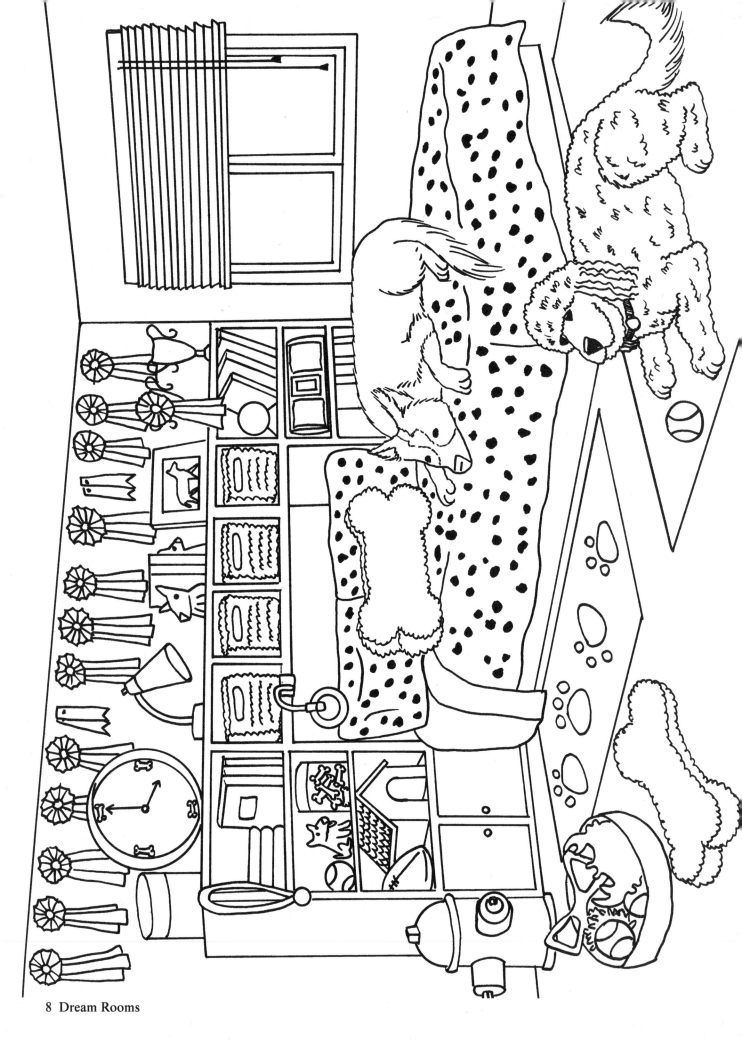

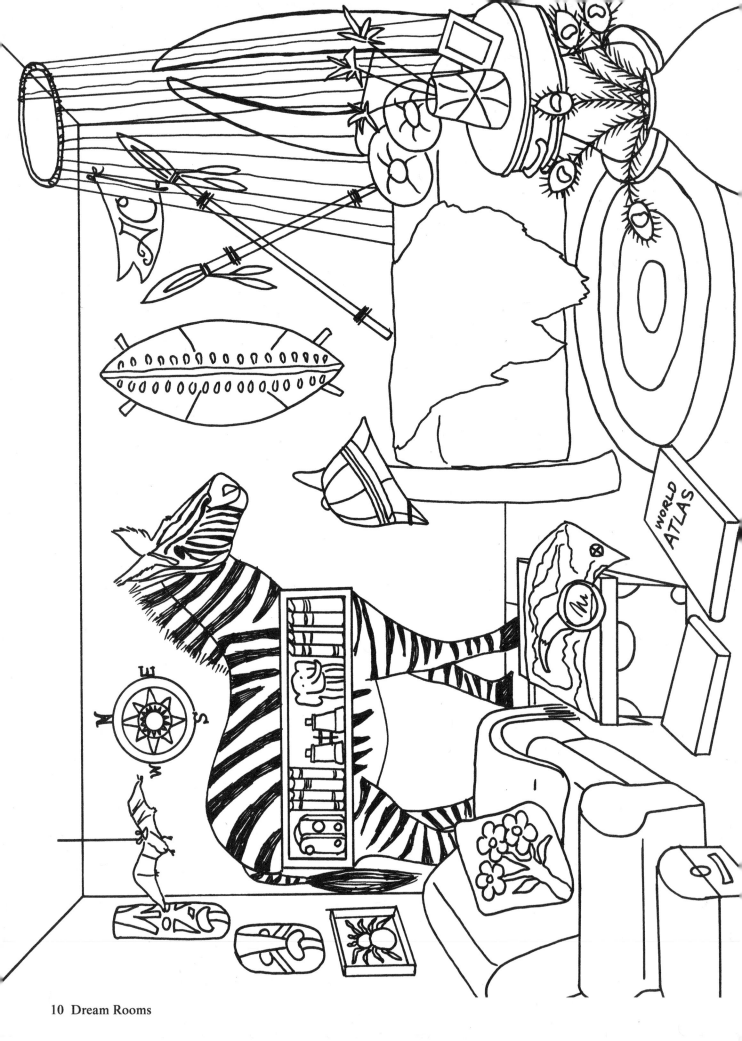

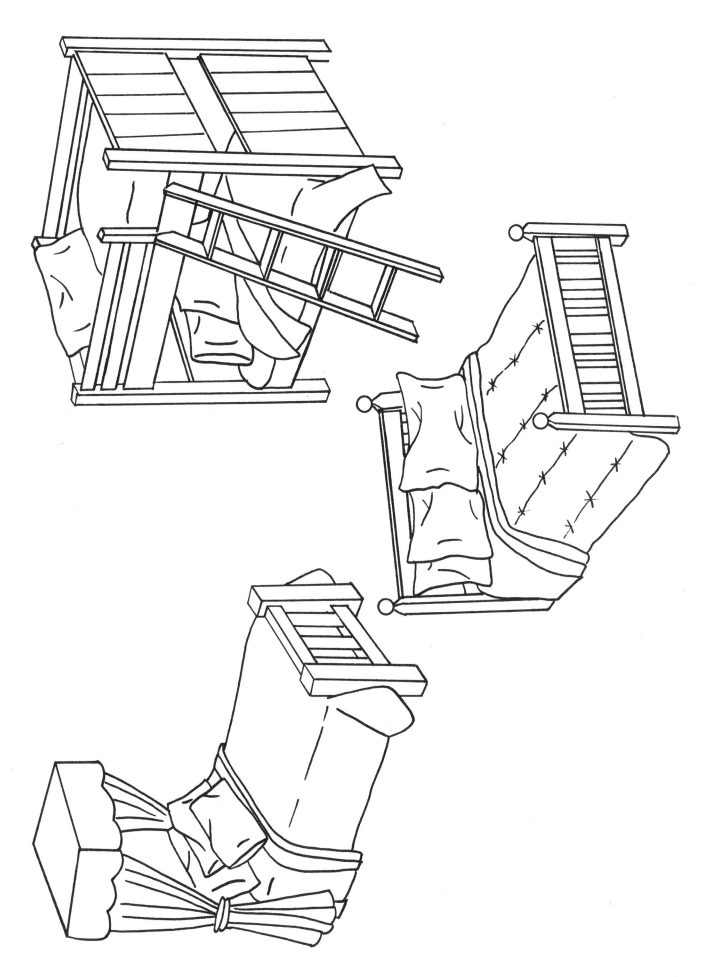

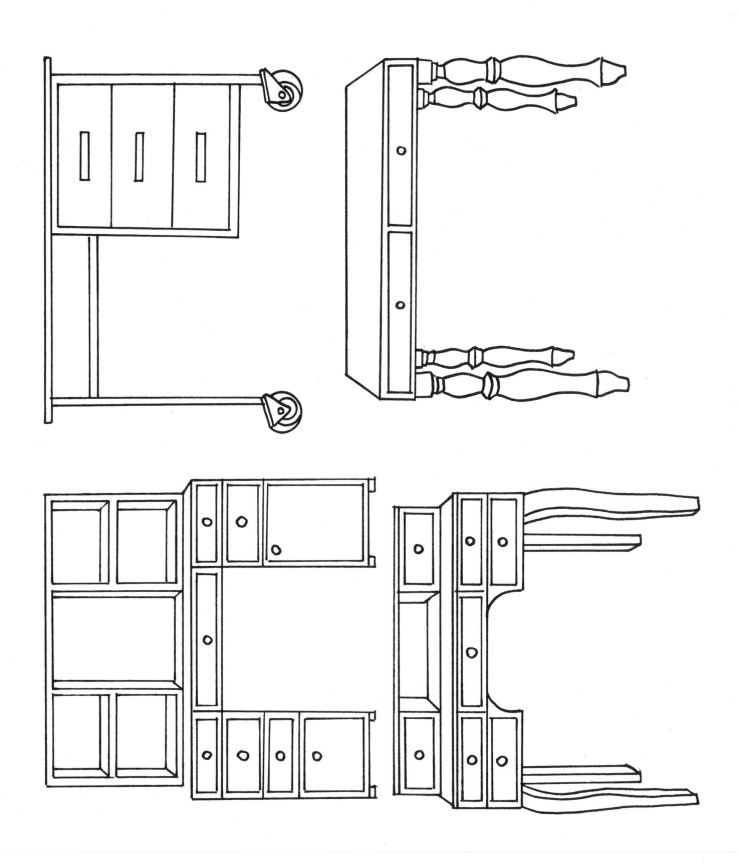

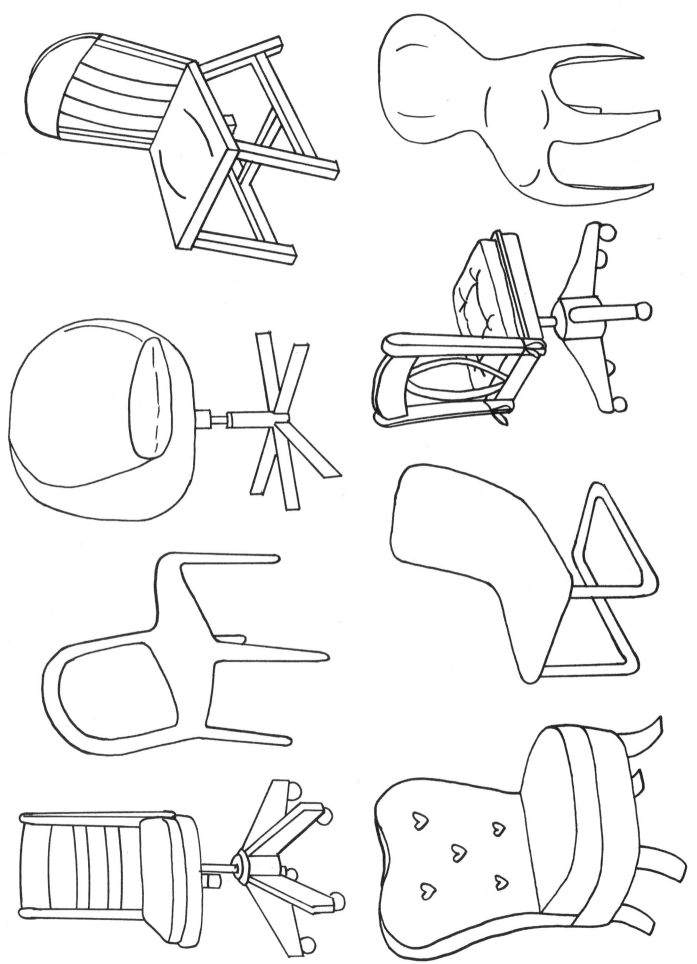

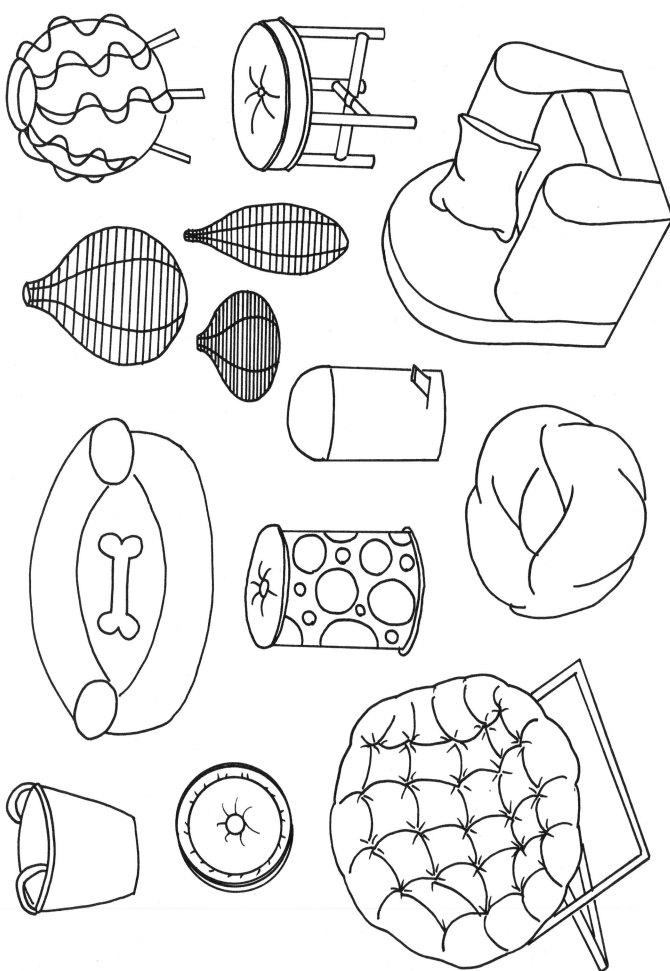

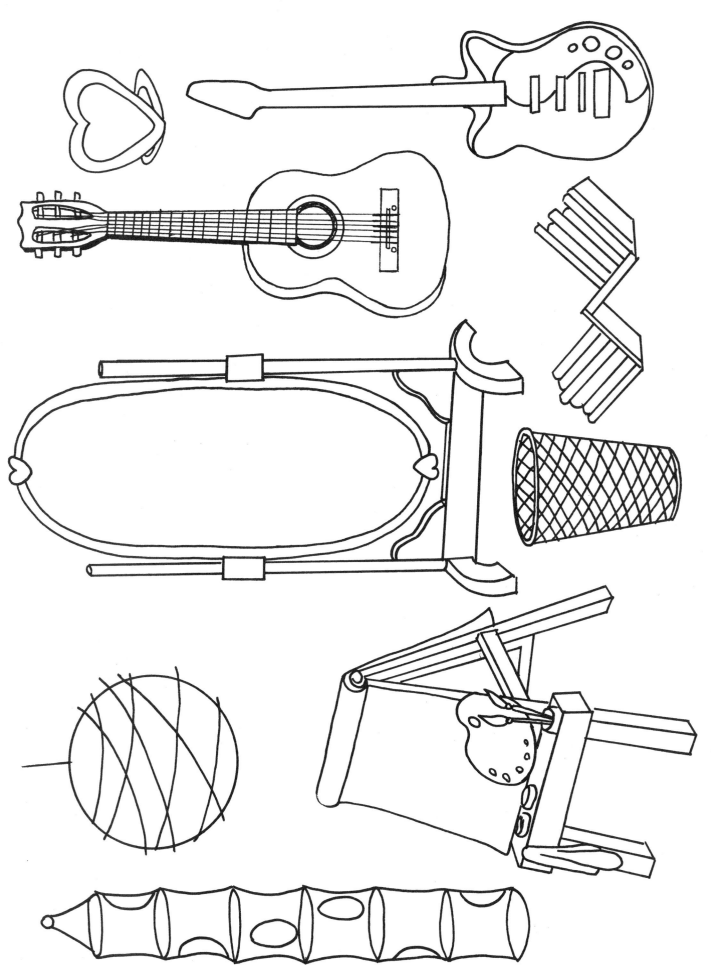

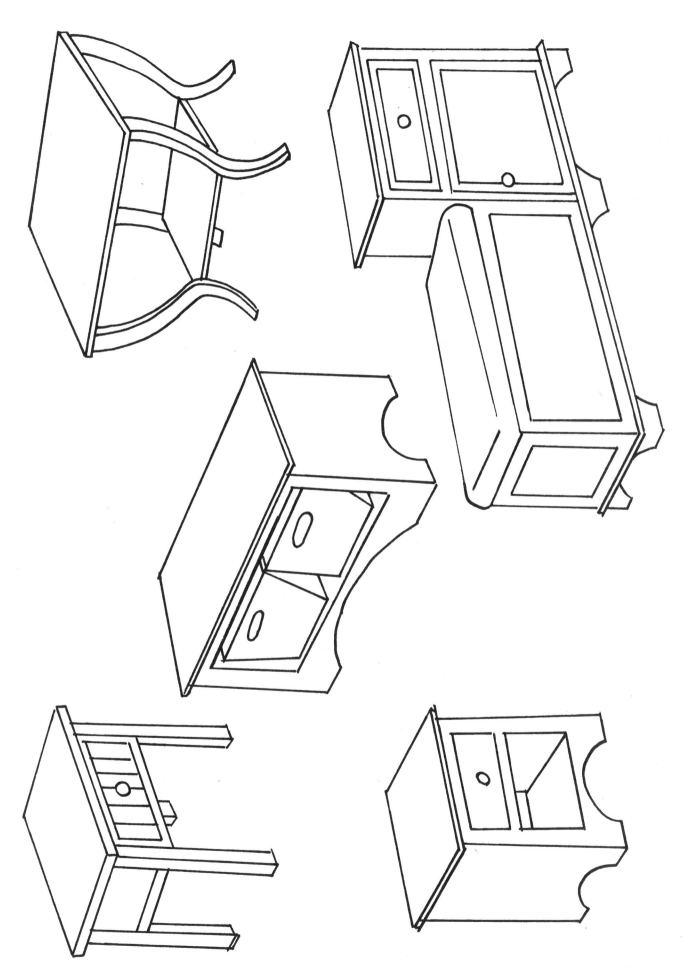

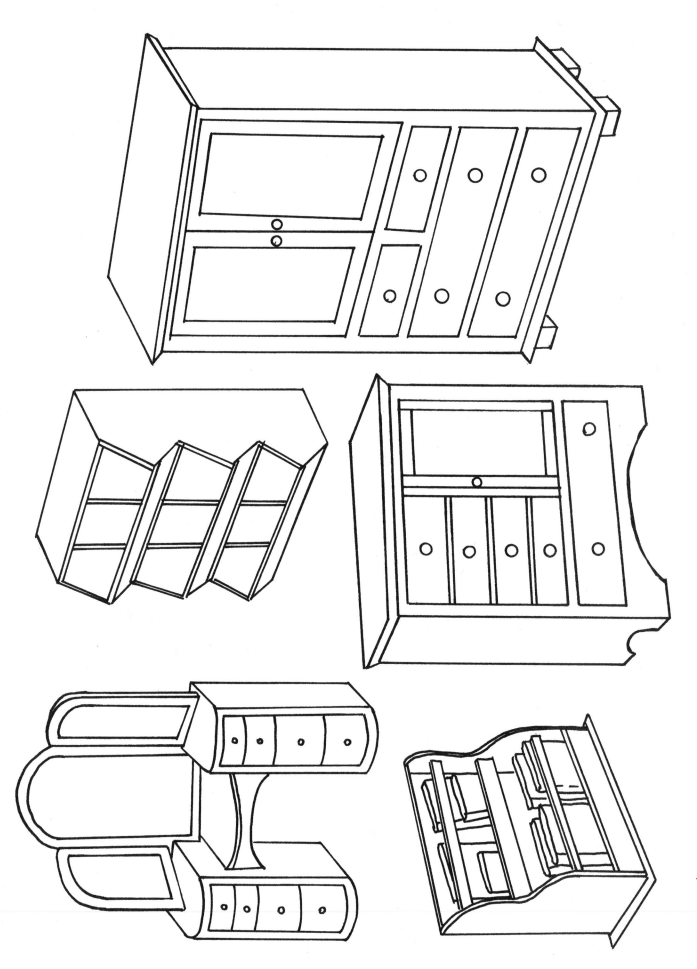

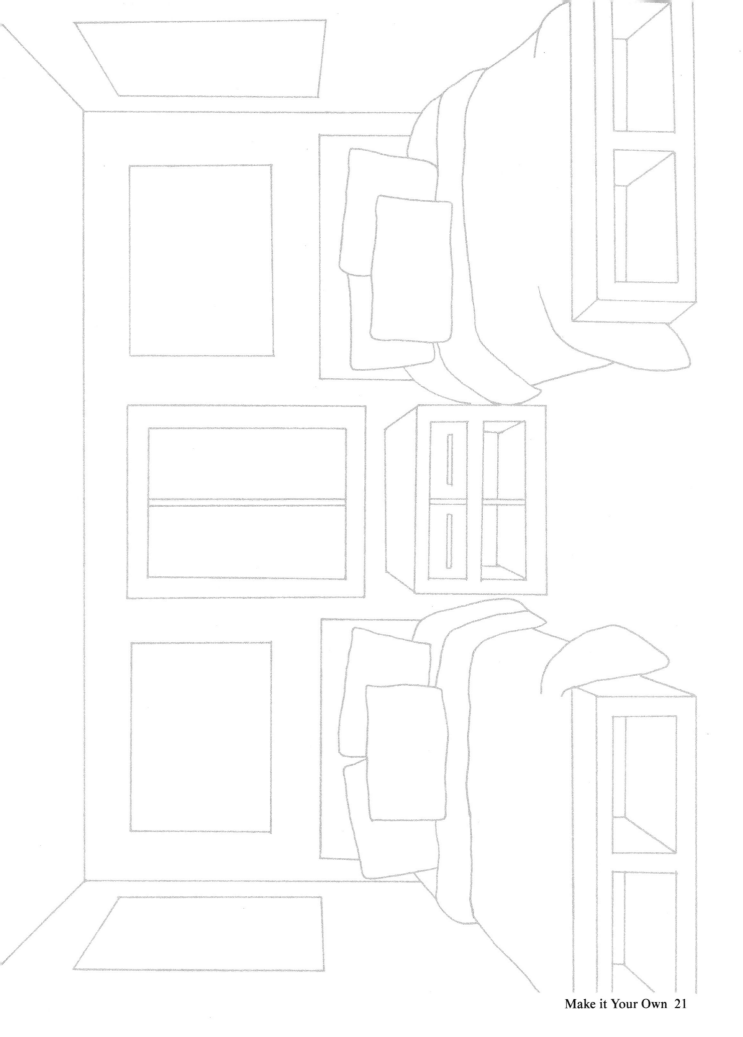

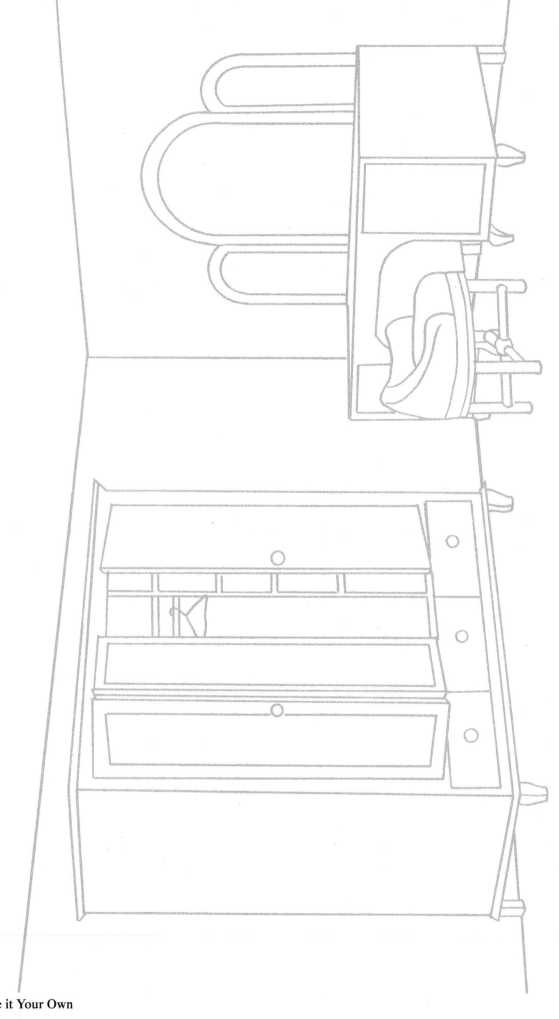

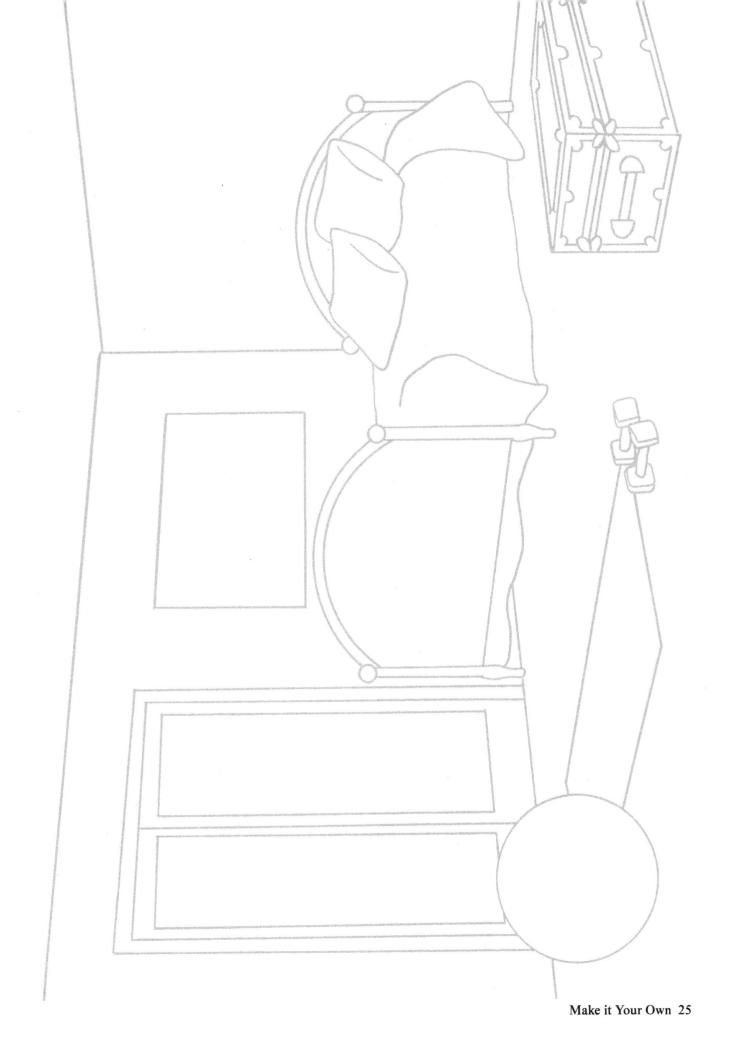

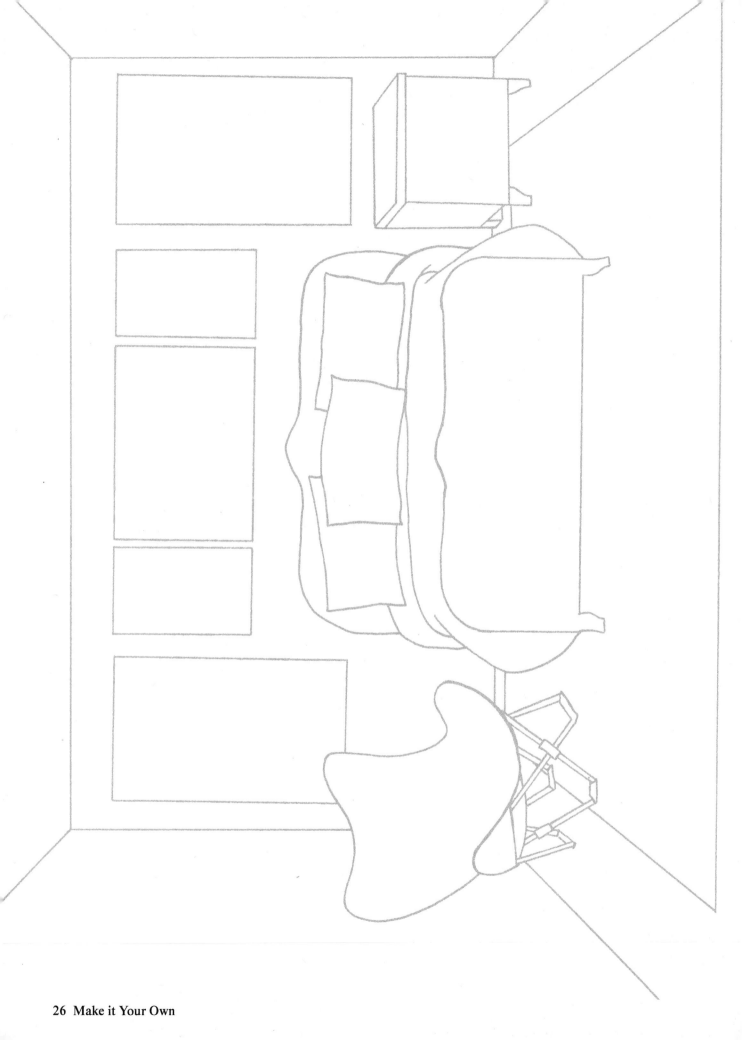

Make it Your Own 27

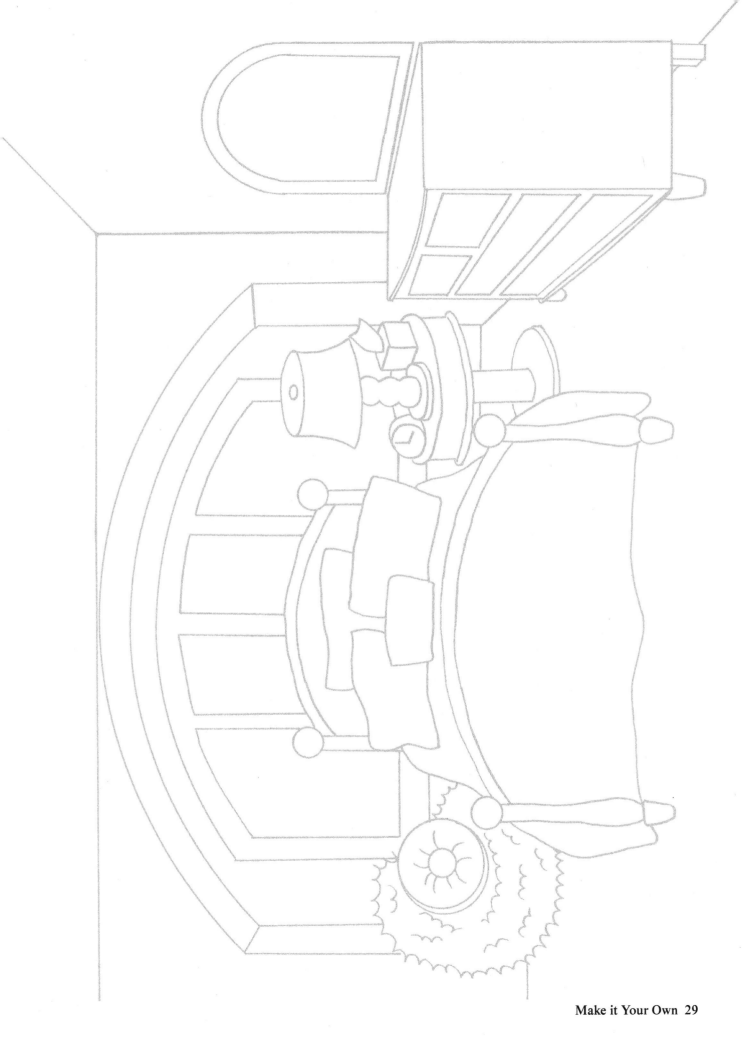

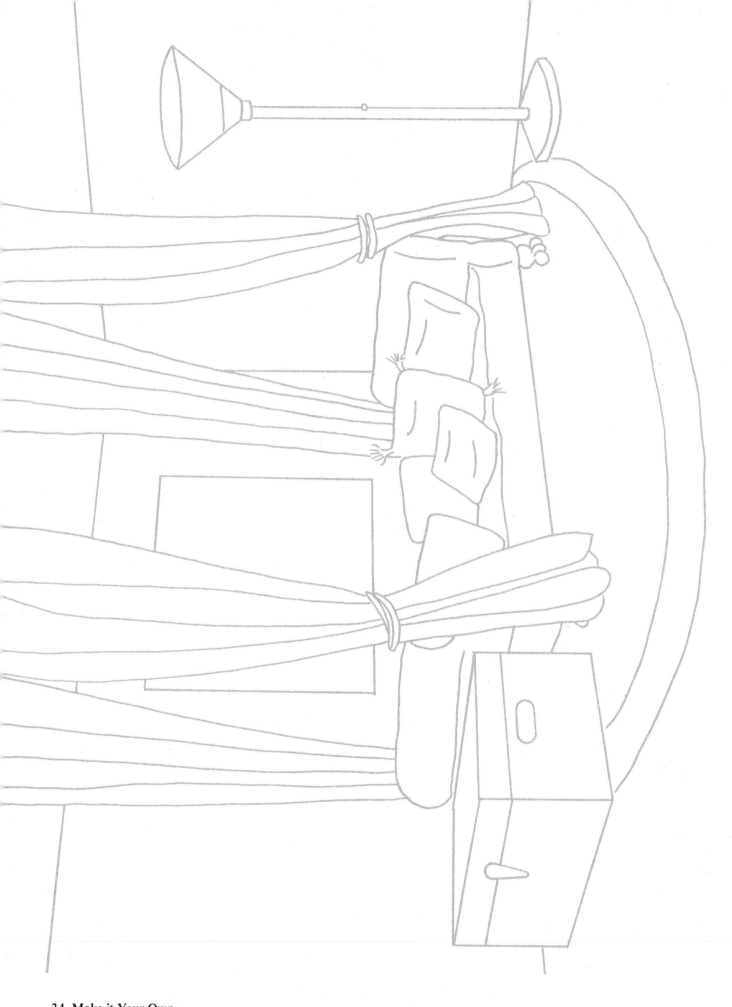

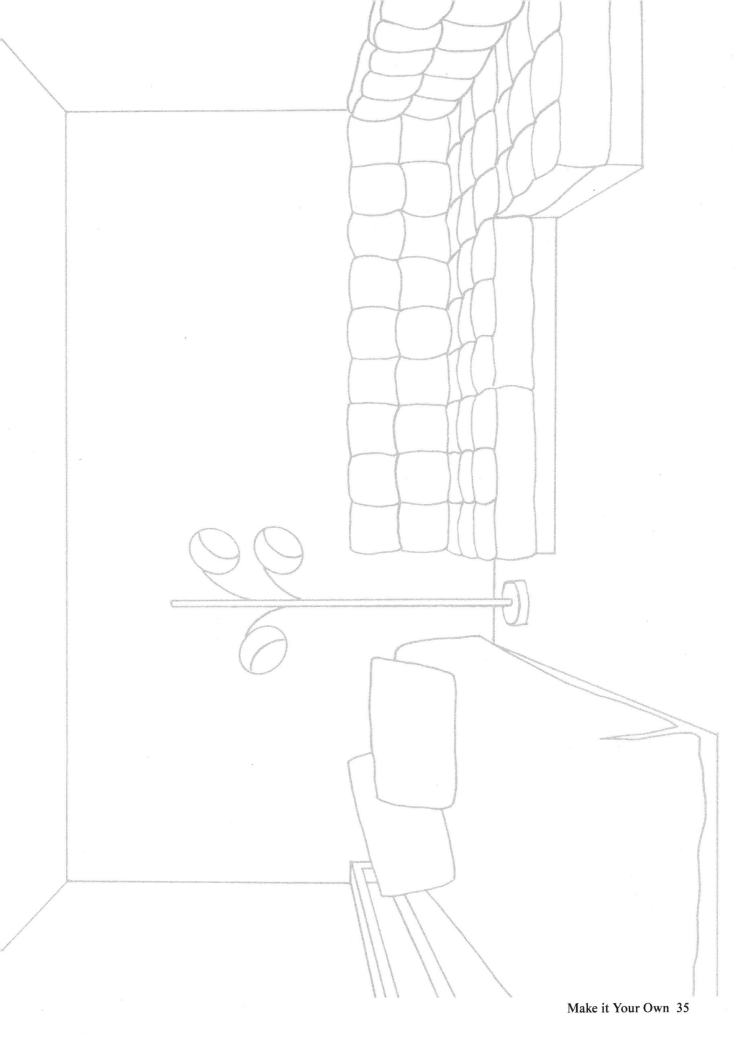

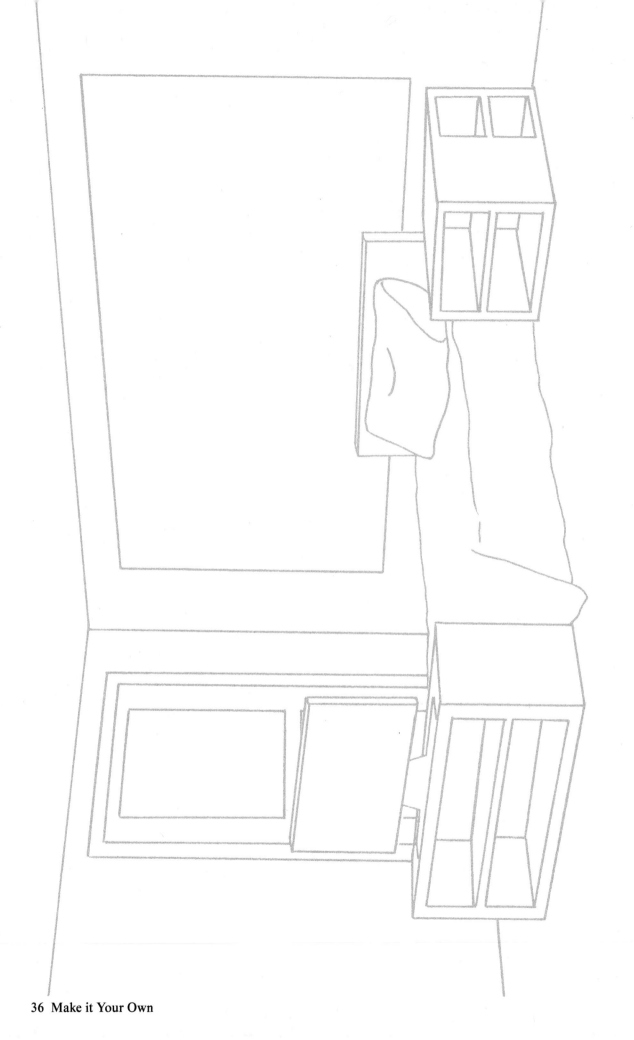

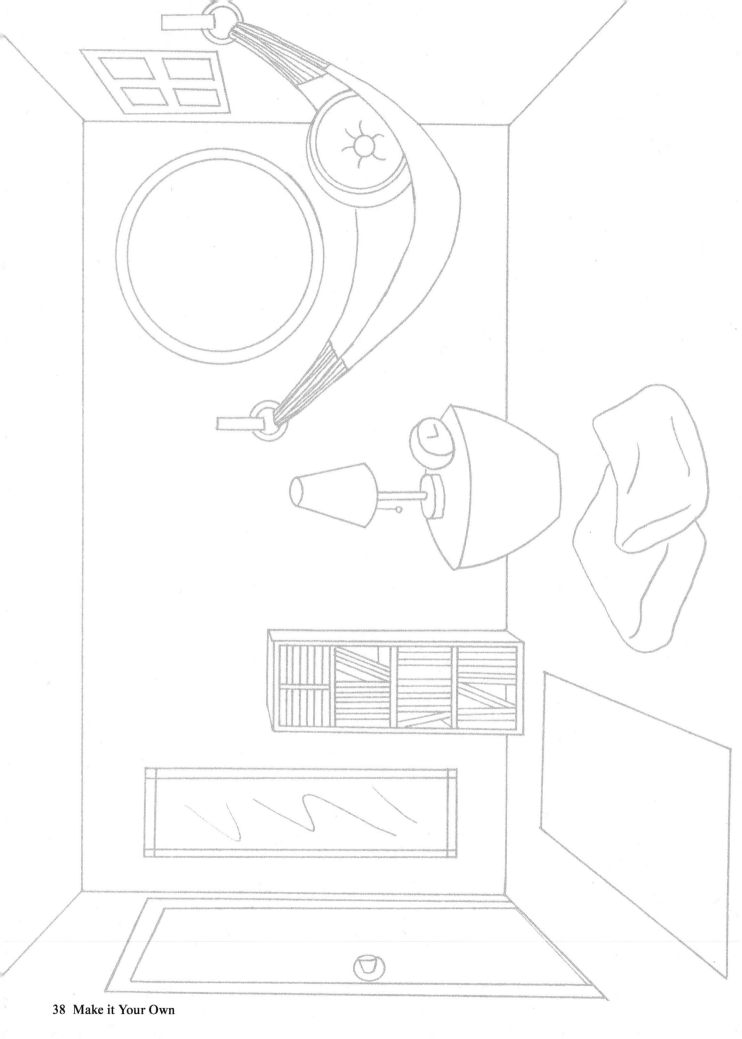

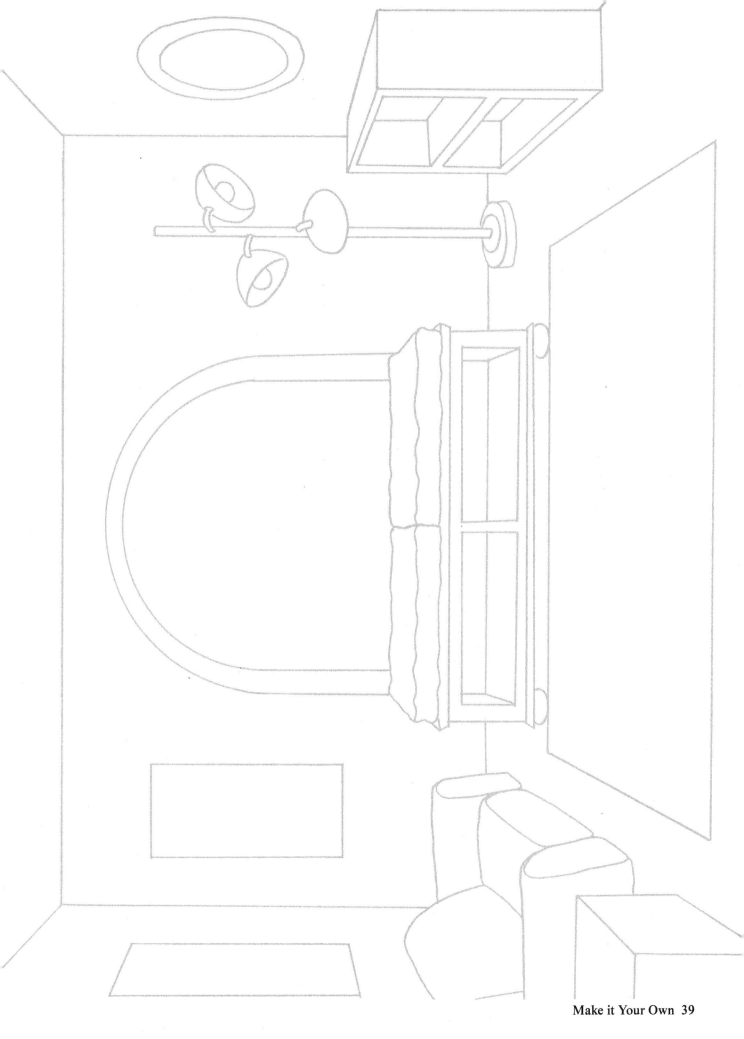

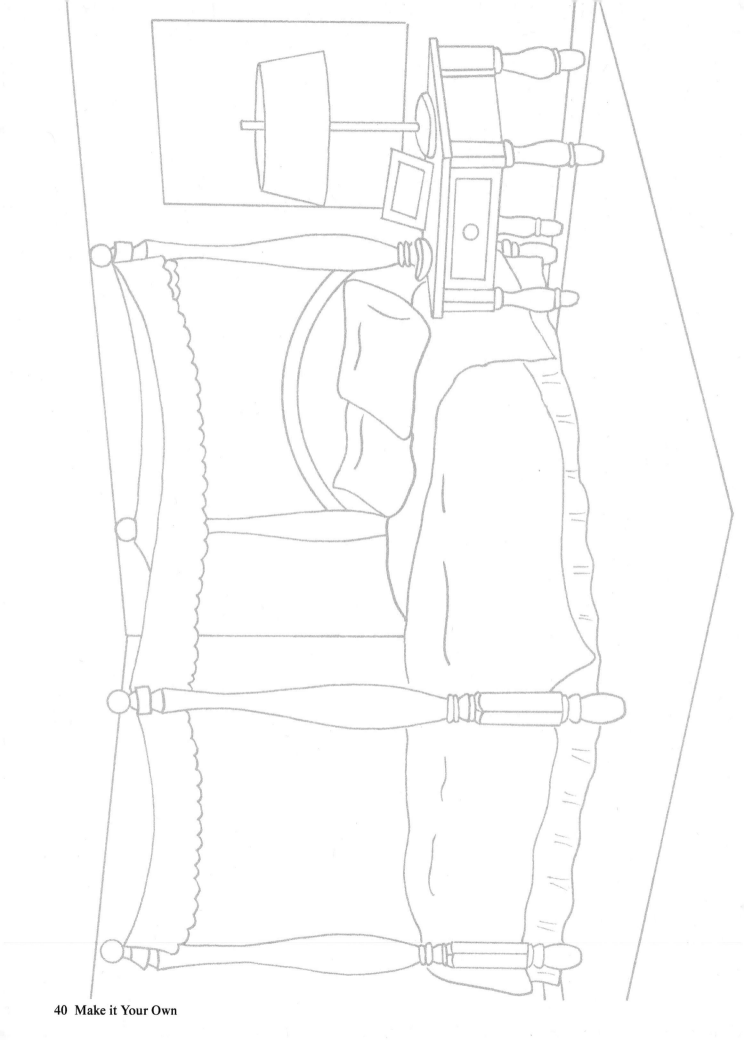

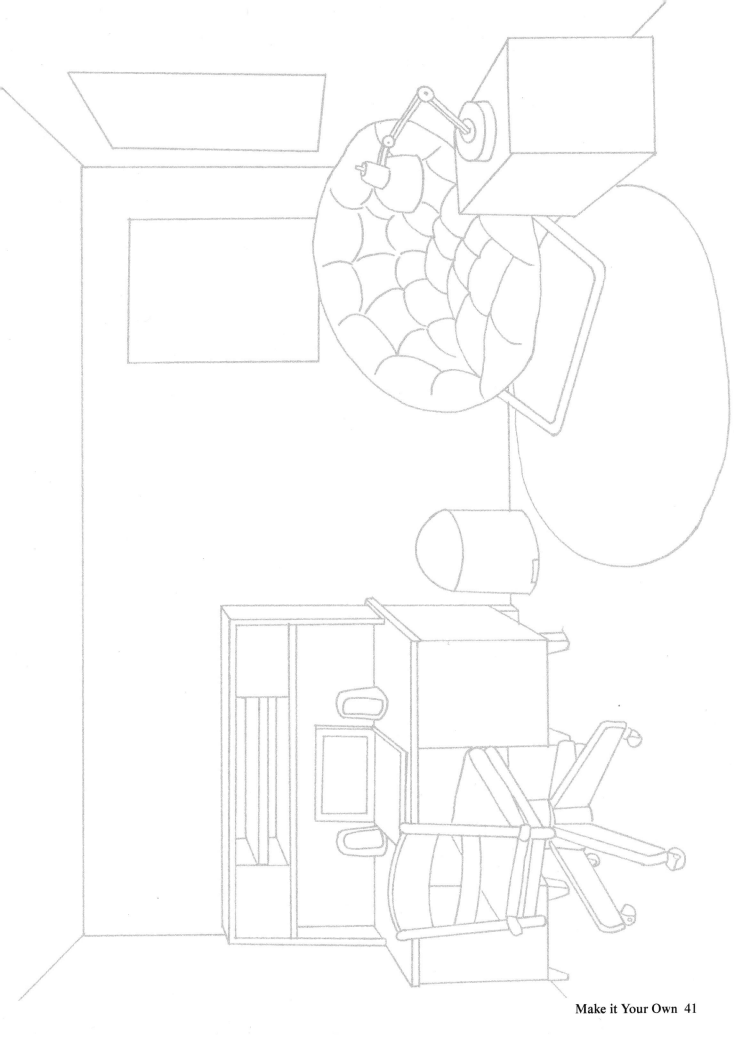

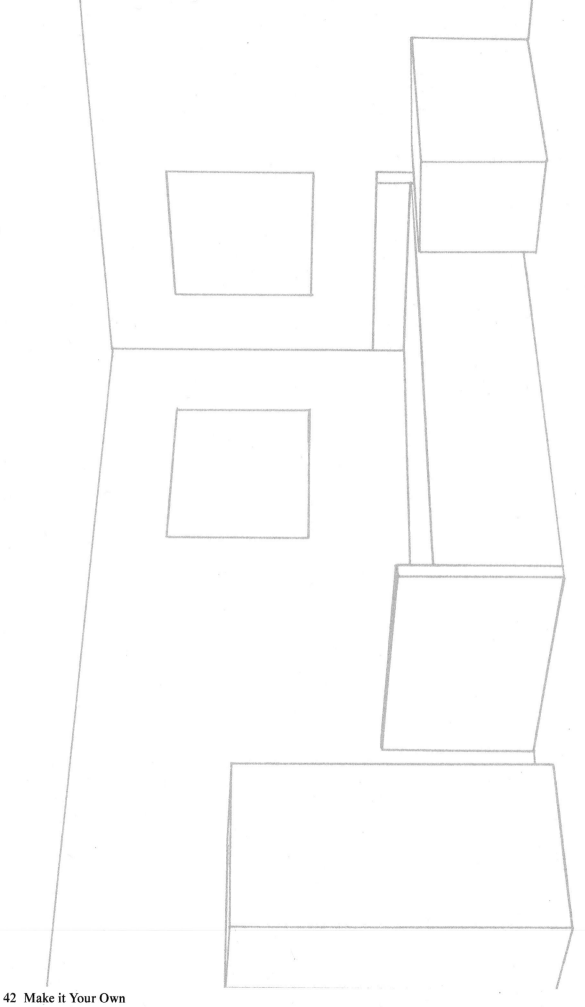

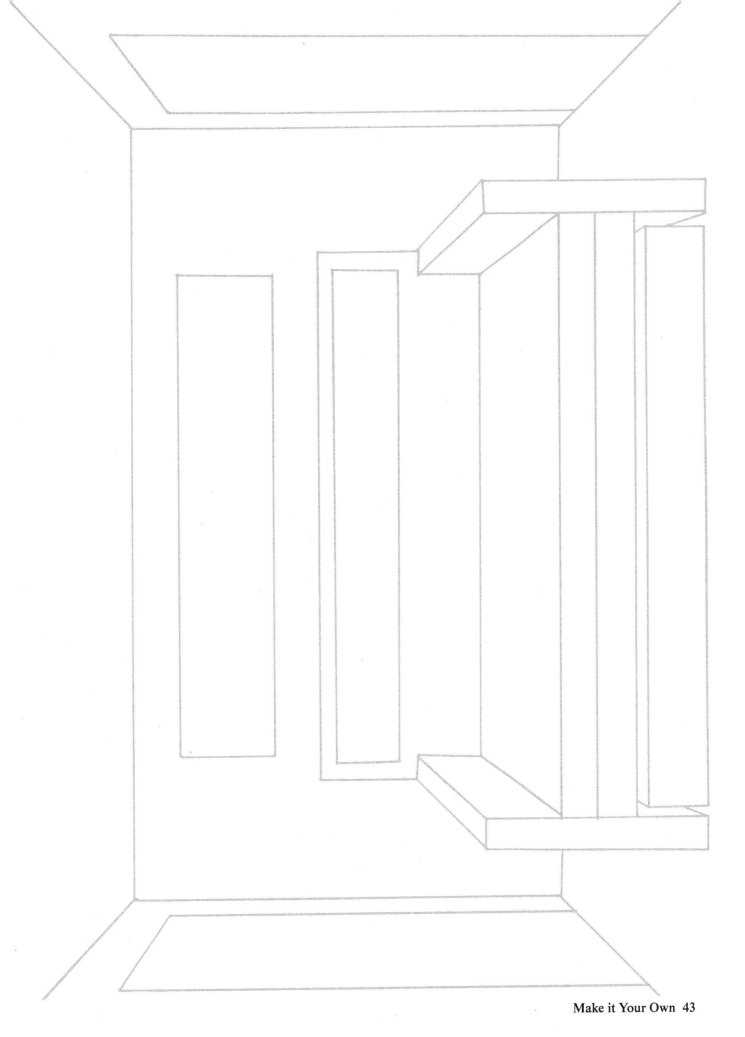

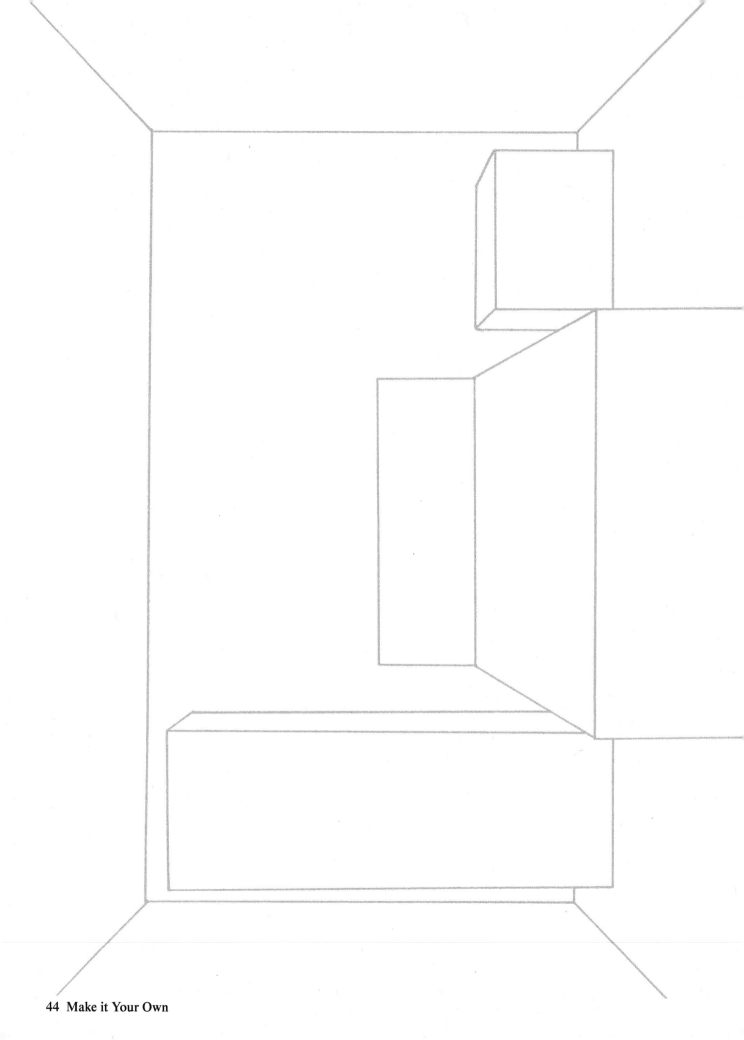

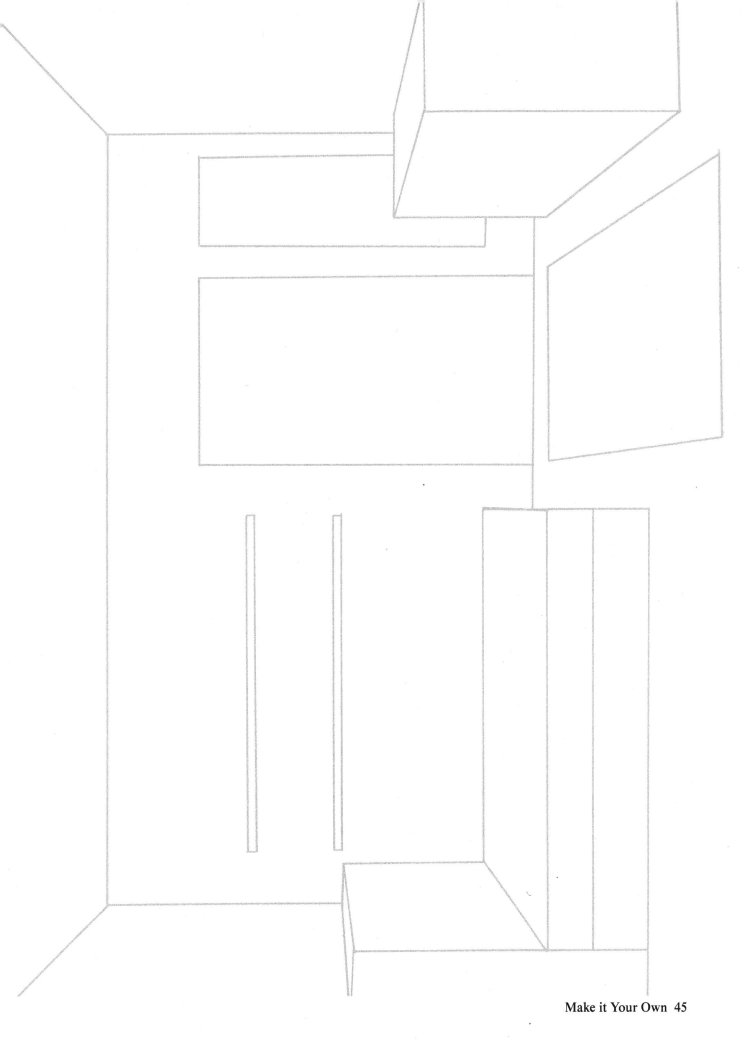

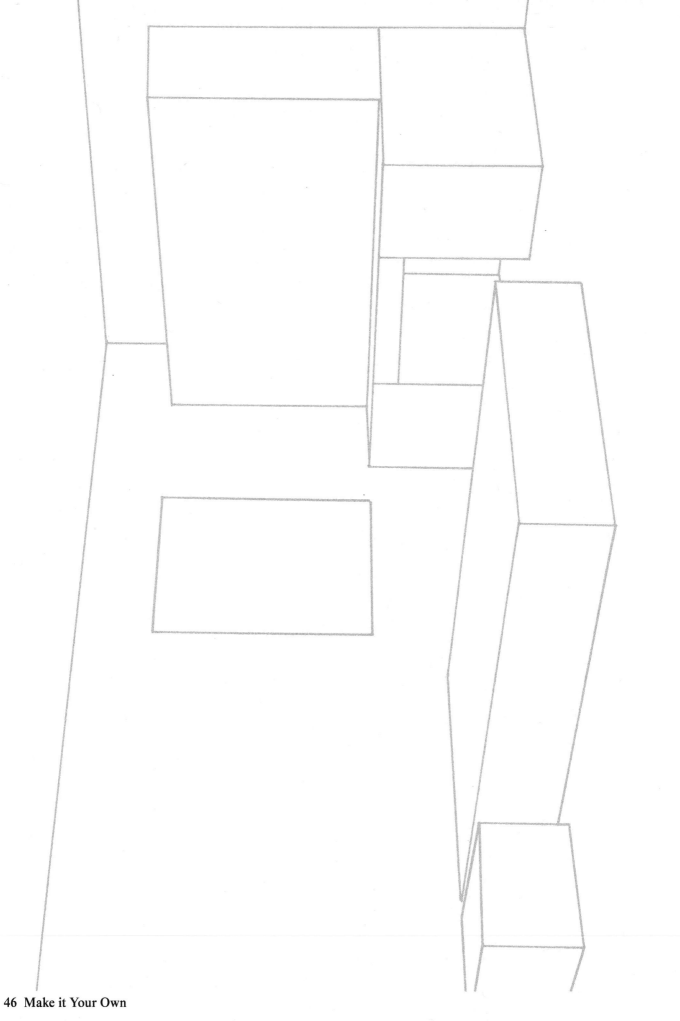

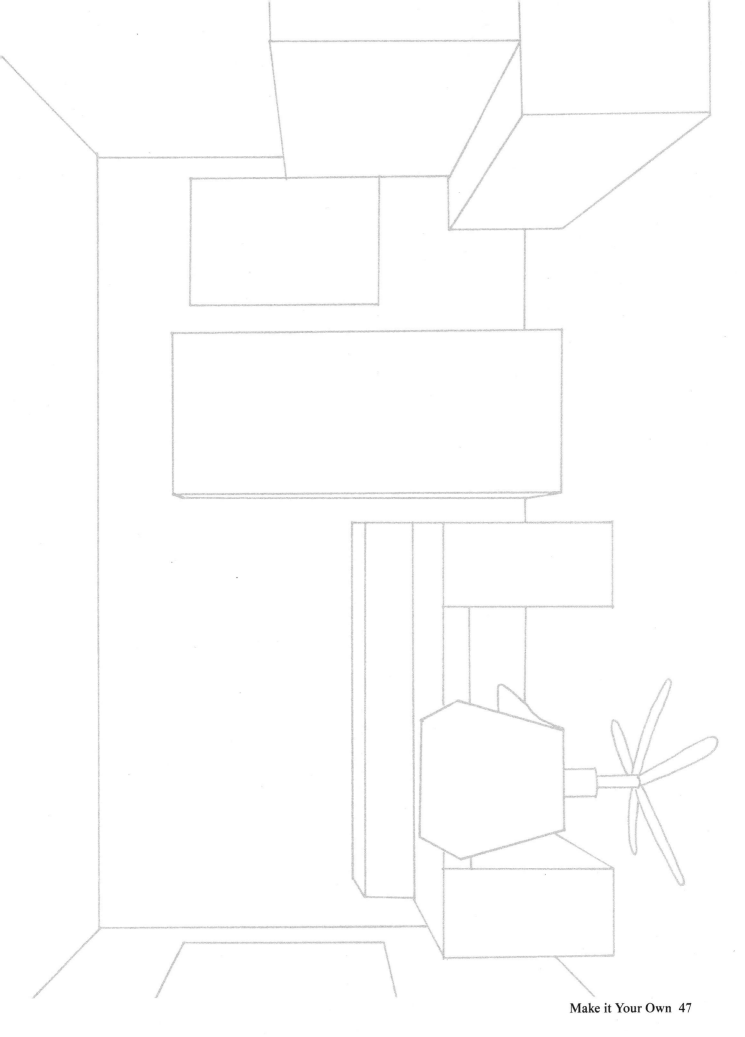

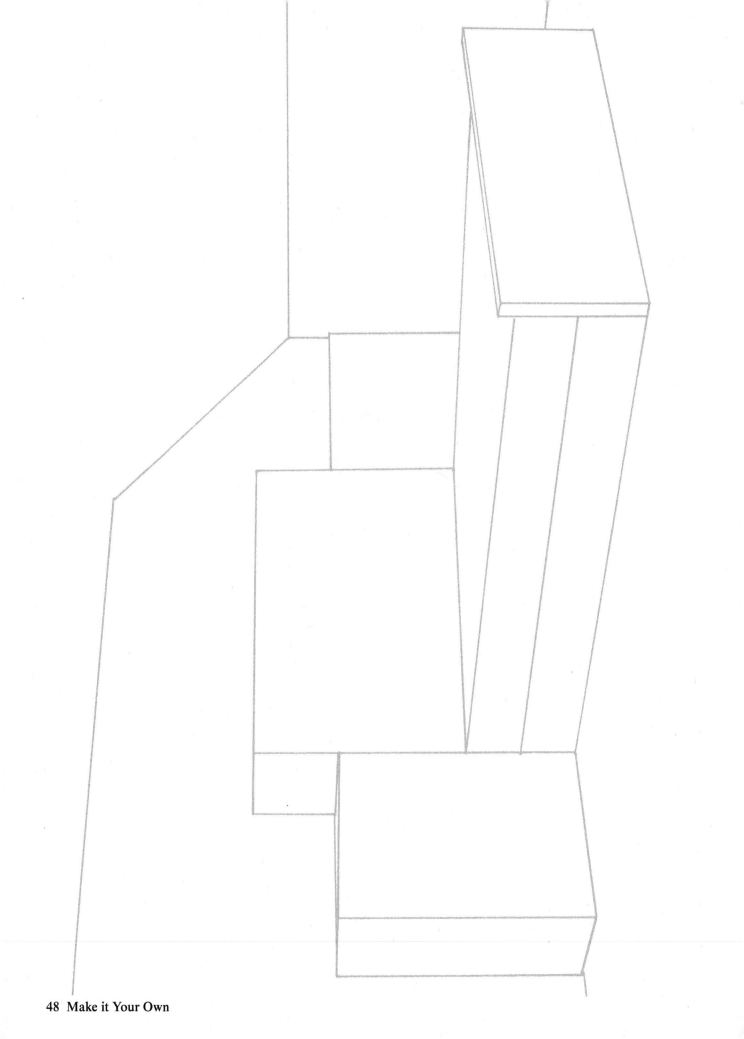

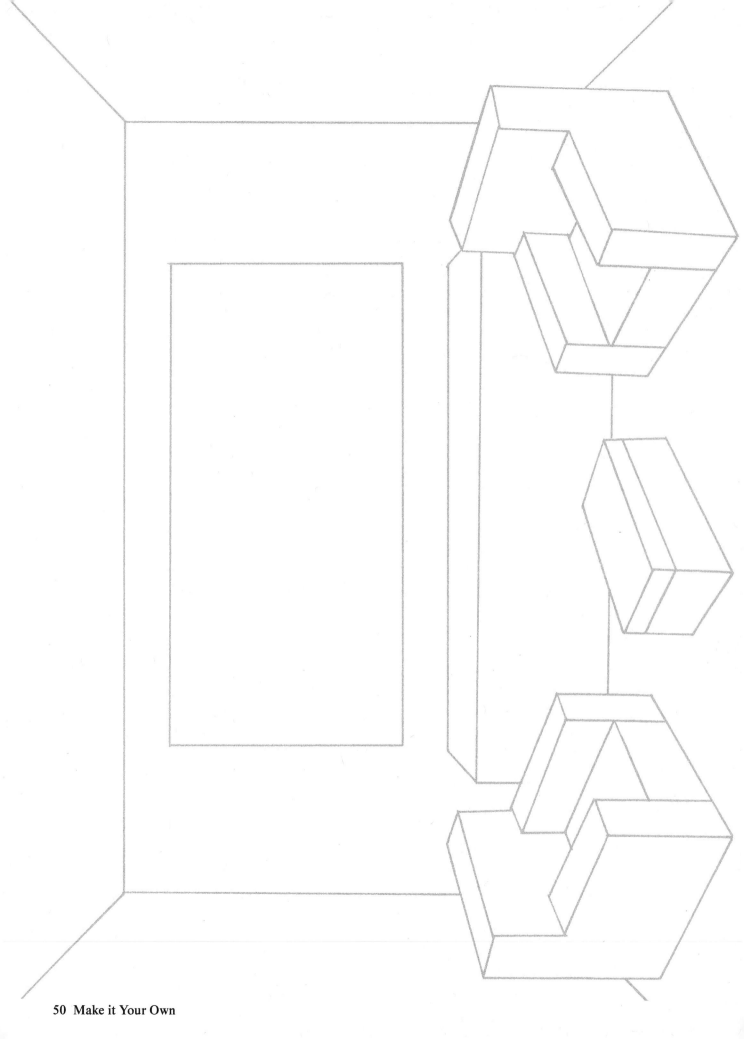

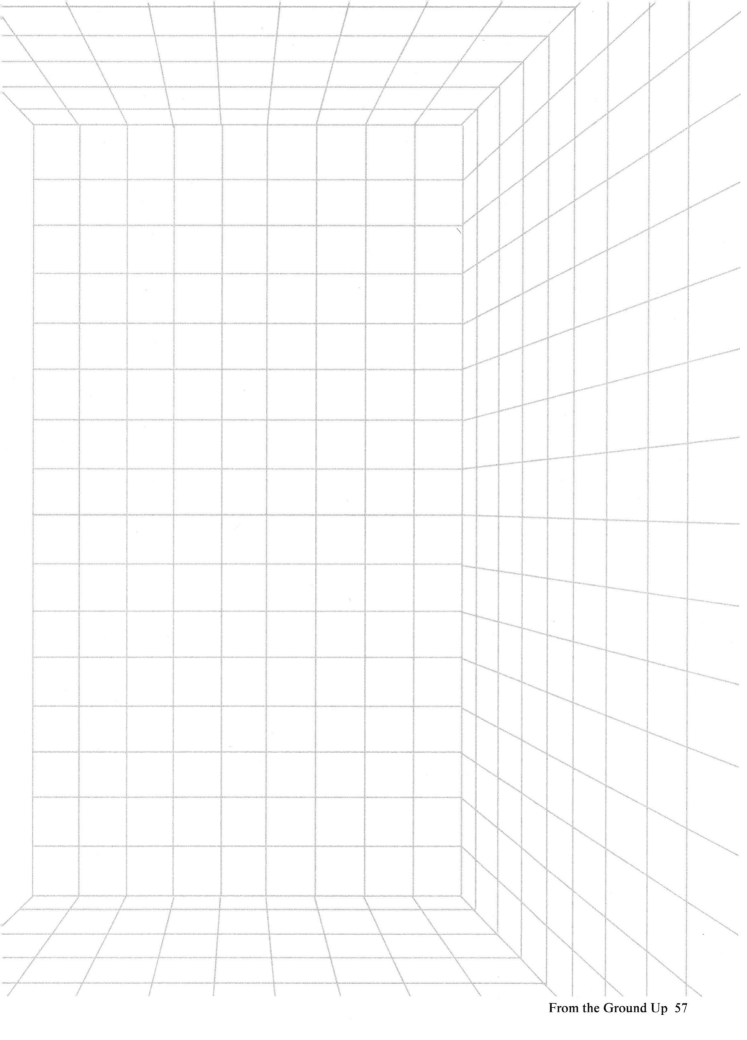

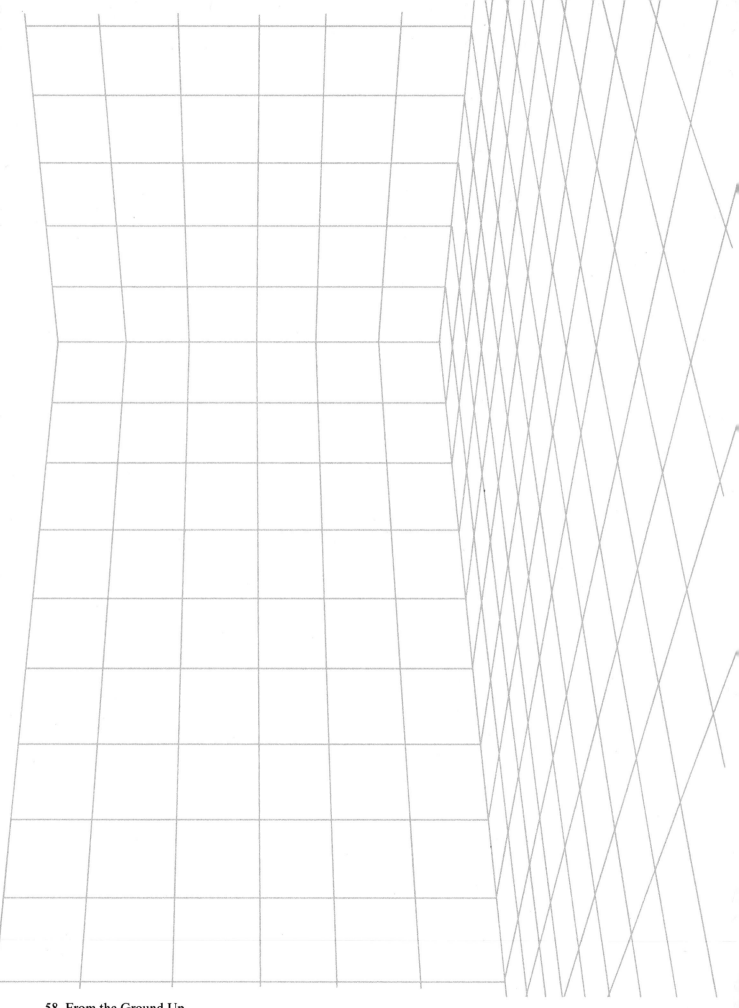

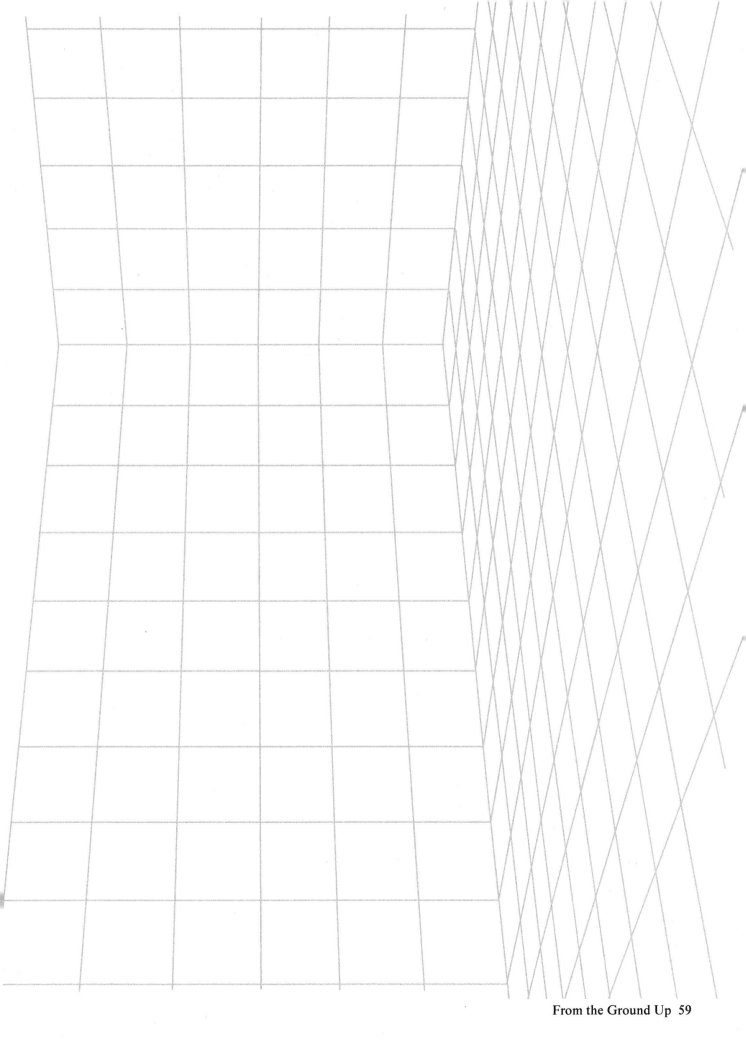

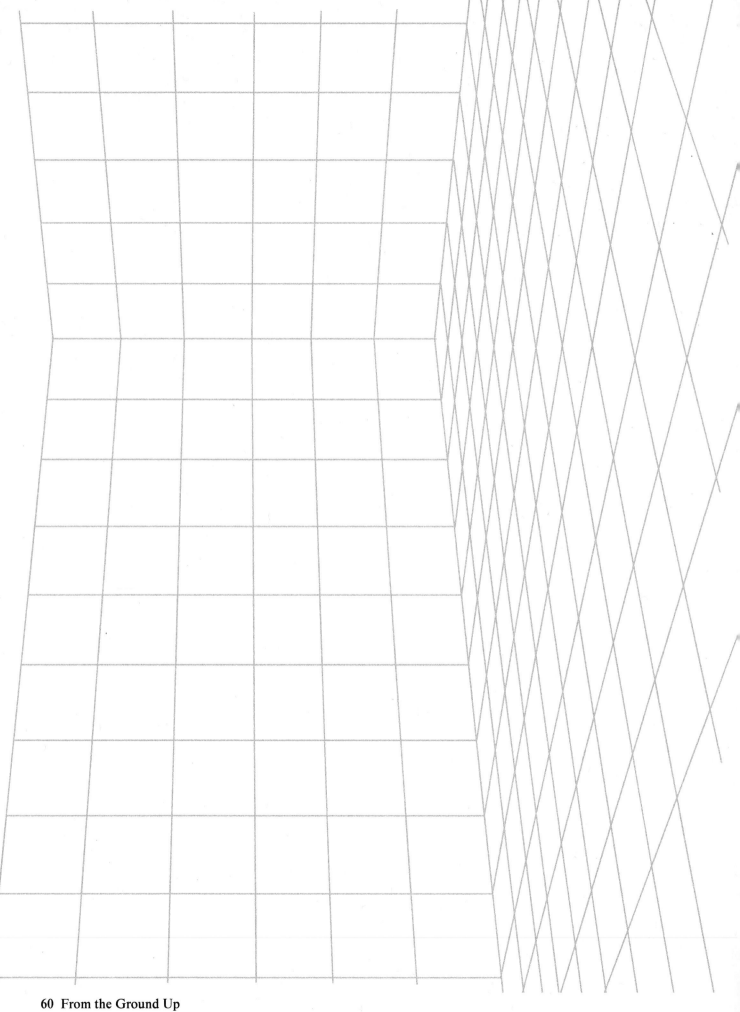

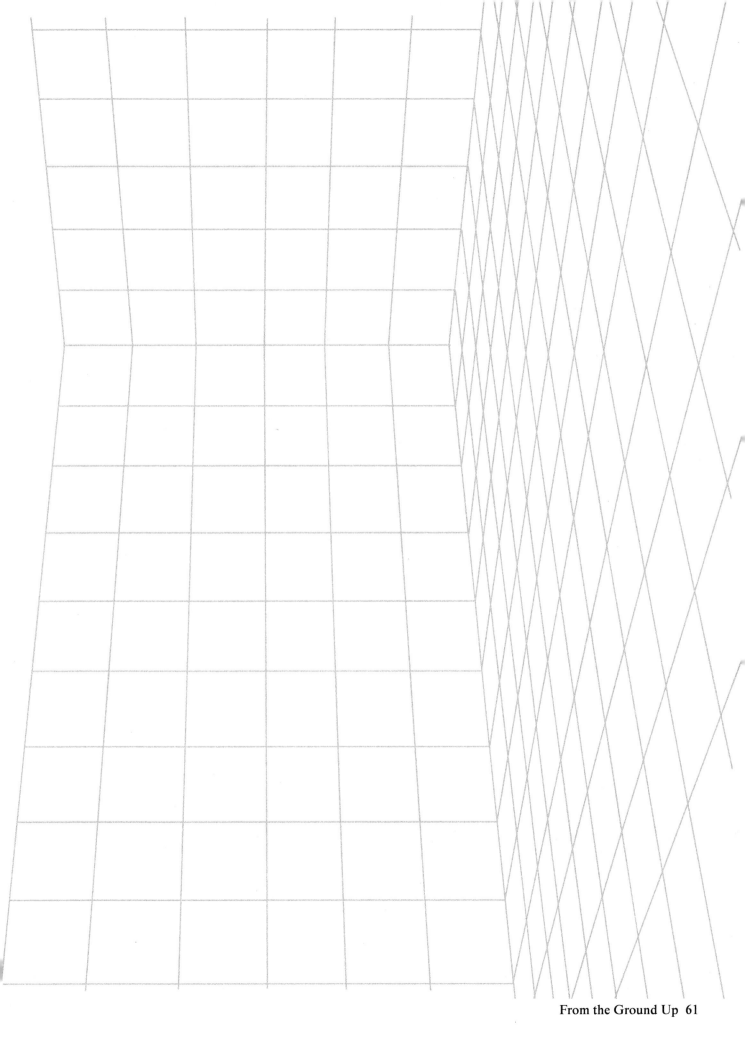

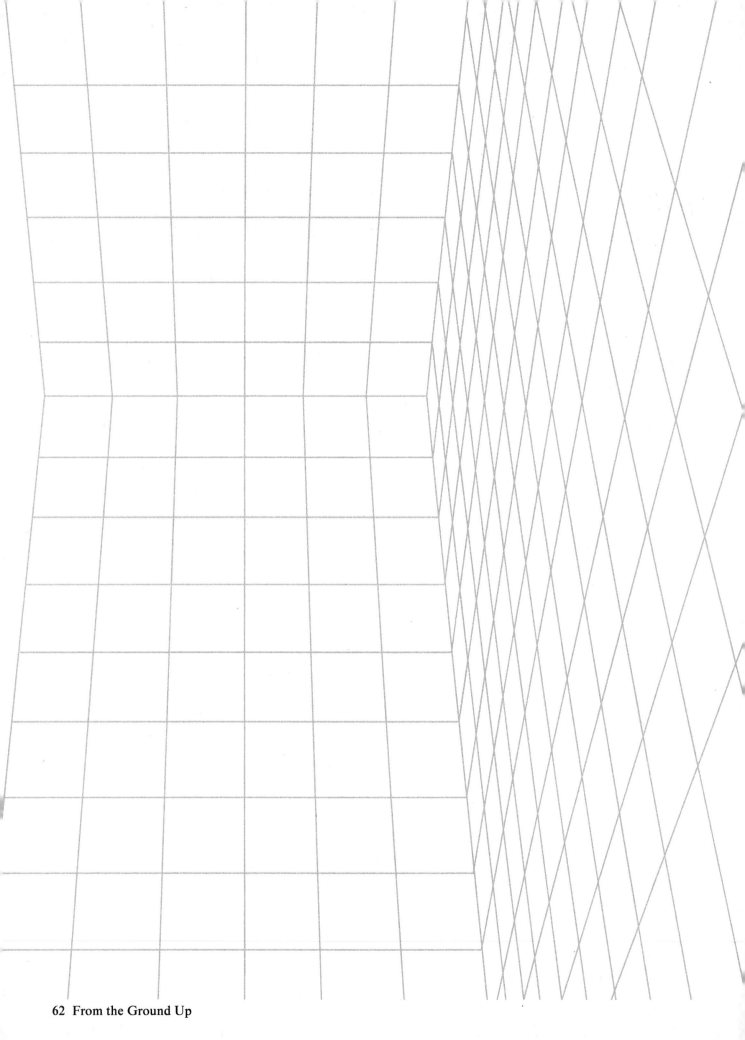

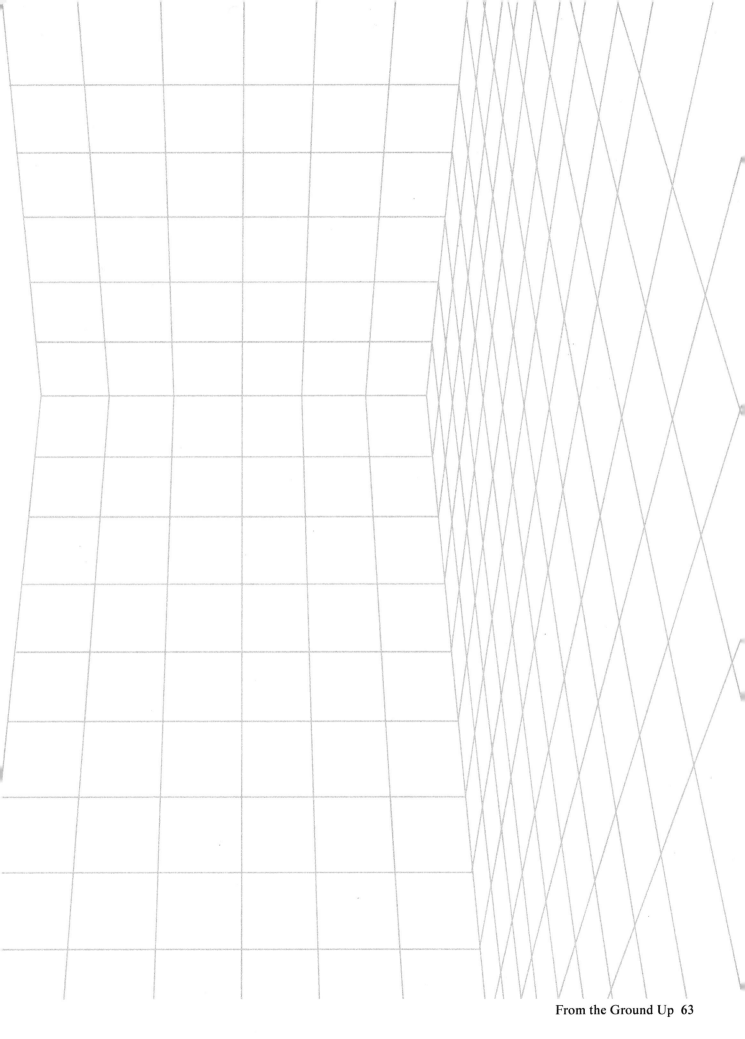

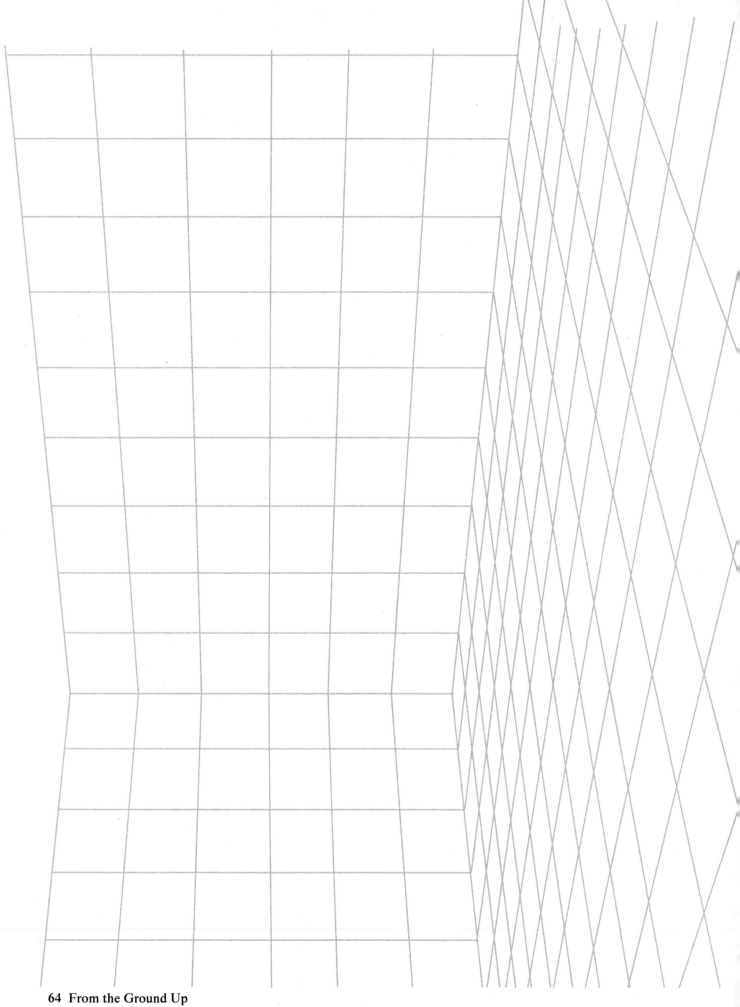

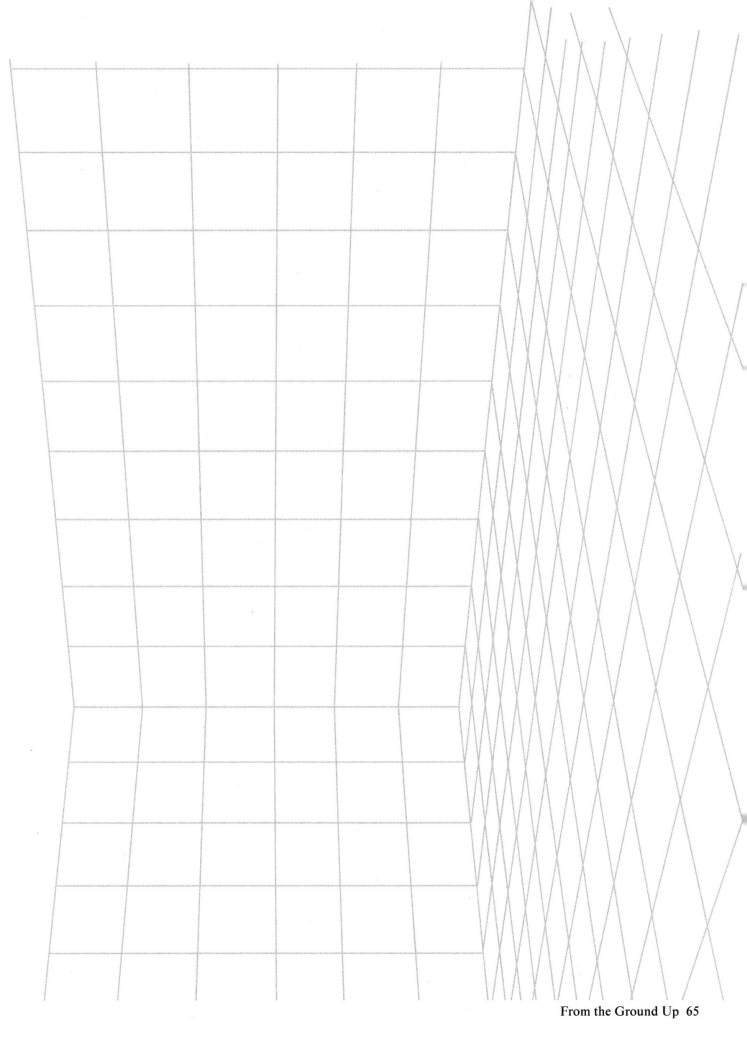

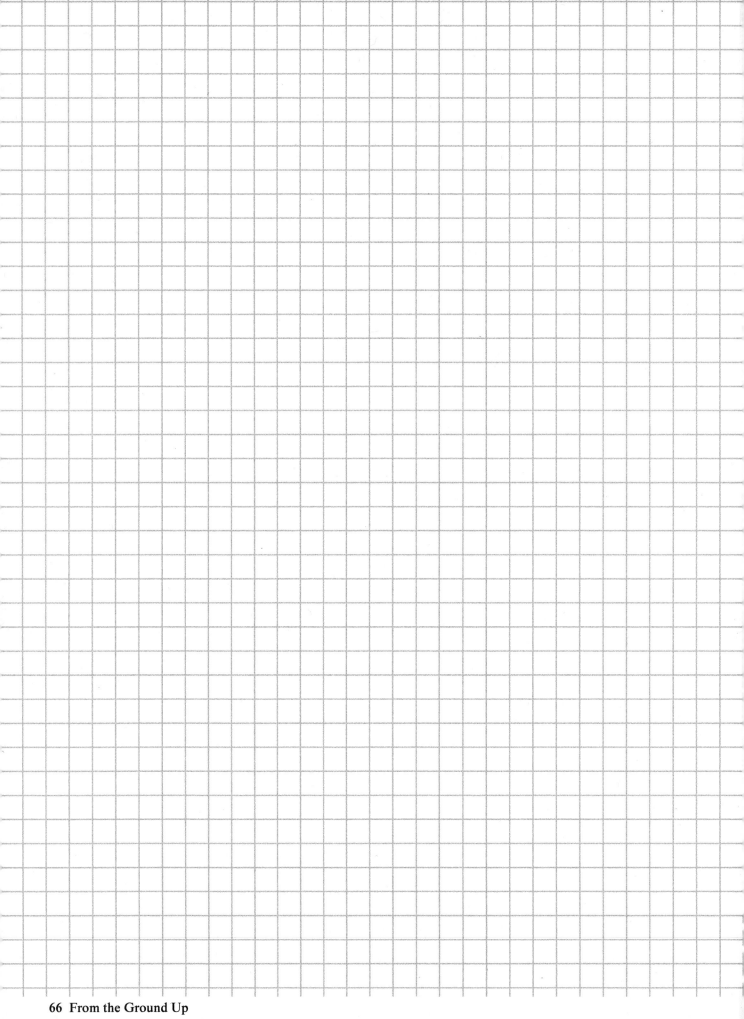